Holiday

Also by Jennifer Firestone:

Waves (Portable Press at Yo-Yo Labs, 2007)
from Flashes (Sona Books, 2006)
snapshot (Sona Books, 2004)

Letters To Poets:
Conversations About Poetics, Politics, And Community
(as co-editor with Dana Teen Lomax, Saturnalia Books, 2008)

JENNIFER FIRESTONE

Holiday

Shearsman Books
Exeter

Published in the United Kingdom in 2008 by
Shearsman Books Ltd
58 Velwell Road
Exeter EX4 4LD

www.shearsman.com

ISBN   978-1-905700-53-0

Acknowledgements
Grateful acknowledgment to *BlazeVOX*, *Connecticut Poetry Review*,
Fourteen Hills, *moria*, *Poetry Salzburg Review*, *Sidereality*, *Sugar Mule* and
Tin Lustre Mobile where these poems first appeared, and to Sona Books for
publishing part of this book as the chapbook, *snapshot*.

Special thanks to Dana Teen Lomax, Sarah Rosenthal and Jill Magi for their
discerning eyes and growing friendships. Particular thanks to Jonathan
Morrill for his unwavering support, generosity, insight and love.

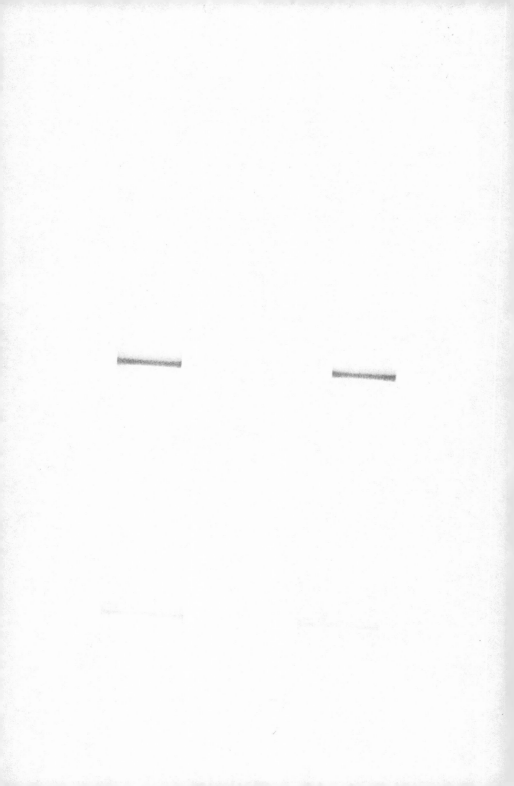

ONE

Figures spiral upward.   Male arm flags.   Ribs, thighs, buttocks.

Architecture.

(I see you carver.)

She shoots from mass.   Eyes swoon.
So smooth.   Sex/violence.   Black
Birds.

Marble stone.   As mirrors.   As pop aesthetics.   As pedestaling.

Push/pull.   Endeared/sickened.
Which is it?
        Precarious times.   [Not fine.]

It was suddenly there
the Israeli woman wrote words down
she was far from water
we were given a camera
to shoot
a couple who entangled quickly
and then because it was
our move
we posed
beneath deflecting pink sun
running toward the edge
you left
slicing at your ankle
blue

I was living it
    unsheathing
    like a thick vine
    between space between
    ribs

The connection
heralded (it was in someone's headlines)

Outside all of you
    knees touching

Lip marks   luscious clouds

Through a window
closer still
behind a line

I want
a
ticket

I want to pay   watch   the movie

Telephone line extends   buildings shade yellow   where colors
mute   where planters

Out of throw-away marble   in a shed   3 years later
biblical figure

Backwards   with left hand   can't read his journal
30 minutes' sleep

I say talent   I say talent   I say talent   is a tall bird creeping

Don't waste a minute   make something   out of everything

The canvas   productive for market   Donatello carves
St. George   advertises him

*Pay for a supper for me and I will make the saints go into the niche
without trouble*

Carte blanche   to 300 figures on ceiling   climb   scaffolding

Proud   to be buried   in floor   paid for   heaven

Making up a holiday
    start by the water
I left first
    straddling the sea

Following the others
    a procession
choose which rocks to see

Over the bridge
    slopes dictate the way
below it shines
    don't stop for reflection

If it's not after this turn
    I failed

Battered sideways   sacrificed to shortcomings
old song collapses from rooftop
pink light on wall
trick of sound   film over cylinder

Green photo
the one you take because of the view
eyes blink at large expanse
land excites you
pictures develop as bleeding colors
no center   identity mute
no where or precise memory
just land   mountains

You can't appreciate habitat   this isn't
in the abstract   it's about personalization   how you felt in
the climate   your niche   the scant road between trees is the one
I took in the big hat day four

                              Take Two:

                              eyes half open
                              scarf wraps neck
                              arms swoop waist
                              flowers at ankles
                              I was here
                              next to the outdoor market
                              its
                              wild-colored fruit

again   again   attention

landscape immensely foreign

white comes to darker parts   holding

brown slices high   higher

again
no walking is seen
if so
the ground remodeled

motion first woke in morning
in rain
the form   distinguishable
despite   low visibility
    each shape had names

tenacity in the undergrowth

clamorous goings

the magnifier burned the pocket
look through the hole

seamless attempts but no openings

quiet little bird you will be heard unforeseen unforgotten
you will hemorrhage

push towards a cold front   it reddens

qualms detected   wear a hood

Sky paints itself behind rusted building   brown shutters open
to expanse

Market's cheap handbags, sugared pastries, boar meat. Photo
cuts off tree—long brown trunk, dark green leaves. Behind
body of another, sea-green shade.

Below shrubbery, sharp green. Against metal fence, turquoise car
kissing silver car, euro brand.

Teenagers with ice cream on steps. The clock struck. Cats
on sidewalk tables. Telephone sign moon-like. Diagrams of
flowers in the shop. Postcards of Leonardo's inventions. A day
of lines. Telephone wires cross buildings. Slim streets break into
green brush. Lantern lights flicker. Rich café. A jump in my
spine.

Free from walls, down trail
past park, tennis courts, ornamented houses. Down aisle,
trees line the way.
Expanse, expanse. Vulture disturbs air—camouflaged
by rocks to the left.

Expanse: wings open. Flight. Dotted hills.
Pink house, white roses, planters on cobblestone walk.
Man in upstairs window.

With sleep, natural water
a time capsule could be
turned up   the possibility
of odds

Two Americans, same dishes   divine, divine   she a
whistle to her tone   the trip of life at 46   sought a
painter   who paints fish   she loves fish   wide and blue
in water   where no one swims   confusion with the chef
who took responsibility for the art   unknowingly   back
and forth   endless talks about   blue gold gills

Old man
washing the same spot
whether it is a dog
or woman
objects are exorbitant

I ain't fallen out of the turnip truck and that's
why I didn't take that room
beard webs to his plate   *I have the smallest ability*
for language-take some words, lose others

TWO

The building   Promise of safety   We bow down
To be enlightened

Tangerine lemon walls   rain glides streets
people enter through arches   open umbrellas   splayed flowers

Walk in twos   follow rhythm that is pre-designed
share a cup   think what others are thinking

      There she is again breathing   always breathing
      ready to compensate
      for all her losses   to vacation the hell
      out of things

The man inside an opening of trees paints on rocks

The green bell half-chipped   etched names
Vincenza y Maura 10 / 10 / 2000

The corridor   the other   cars everywhere
cylinder buildings belly to center
how can we fit through tight
space (logistics) and with our automobile
our own

A pale brick wall appears   baby Jesus
and Mary with black hair   dark skin   necks disproportionate
to bodies   sloping lines form shoulders

      Run to the book
      down a stairway
      gray cement against thick skin
      the scrawl mine but
      letters unrecognizable

Church bells broke waves   it was circular
today are prawns with heads ripped off
to get there follow red markings
but the group wouldn't settle our fears
so we ended up the hill
scratched
lizards and hummingbirds watched
on top there was a highway
in the tunnel in fast motion
I sang opera
before, I walked above the train station missing you
fell into a man who blocked my way
after prawns on the cobblestone street
in the middle
the plaza contained dancing
full figures unabashed
took the floor

Crucifixion stark   delicate trees motionless fields   the cross
a monument in the middle

Michelangelo deep Christian
pagan love
of body

        Weight of body held by
        gowns
        stagger to this sorrow

                sorry

Michelangelo
despised painting
"fit for women"

What sick game this smell is suffocating   move your
body away from   the stairs look for the signs entrada
entrada   blur   I've got one hour give me ceiling
groups   cameras   if I must look up

To find the visionary line, perspective, draw it to any item
and tell me about   relation
if sacrificed what will be offered

Gates of paradise
can't get richer
Corinthian pillars
people on steps
a herded animal
the sun a roar

Medieval towns
crowded   unmysterious   hills and hills   and buildings

San Gimignano
approach it
over land
cold brown towers
"medieval Manhattan"

Yellow building   pink flowers
too much the same   makes you feel difference

Squash in shrubbery
wheat
leaves shake
walk down trail
frog lay dead
walls stained wet
building faded

Statue of fertility
in trim of arch
statue split its legs to fish tails
figure holding snaky ferret
crocodile sea horse nipping another's ears

Long polished table   a person at each end

There was the accident

Stop jolt to be continued

Crash clink of glass

Book of listings beneath me   align pages with pen

Bed drifts mid-air unsuspecting

Certain items a person cannot share

THREE

A bicycle treading the piazza
light filters in from tops of buildings
swerves of mortar and cement
initiate the offshoots

The bicycle followed
that same dry noise
scratching the streets

Lost from the hotel
ending at the duomo
uprooted from the ground
scraping in air increased
not making linear connection
thinking of an omniscient bike above all

"You are far away;
we hope they weren't involved."
Michael hounded by reporters.
He told them "since we don't know anything yet
it doesn't make sense to point fingers. When we retaliate
we should make sure it is judicious and measured and
doesn't harm innocents at home and abroad who are
mourning our loss."

"Everyone was someone's baby.
The U.S. as we've known it.
Una will know a different country."

"Kinko's closed and phone lines down all day."

"Across the street there is a bar,
a guy got shot in the head.
Played cards with grandma and Sally.
The second time she is crying."

Rivers wash away most except a ream of tufa that remains.

You pushed me to the desk man as we rode to the room.
The window painted shut   luggage took
floor space.

Carved on its exterior the world sprung from a rib. Arms crossed
in sleep. Twines of branches etched in stone above his head.
Two angels converse. Trees become small like bushes. She fixes
on eyes of almighty that he must take one hand and prop
her head, hair falls toward rock's peak. All bodies physically
the same. No means to mirror a reality. The angels and gods
are dressed. There are birds, lions, horses, a ram.

After, eternal flaws.
Bodies roped together holding faces, ears, stomachs,
eyes sunk, mouths open, heads too big. Devils lecturing.
Bodies on the ground underneath feet. Bodies to the side,
straight forward.

Inside
Signorelli's Last Judgment, round buttocks, muscular thighs
trampling foreign deserts with skeletons and heads. A war above
and many look up to see. Winged devil carries disturbed
blonde on his back (known to be Signorelli's ex-lover). Demons'
wings jut up as they grab angels' dropped horns twisting
the necks of people. The close line between what could be
pleasure. Bones collect as a choir. Many shoulders thrown back
many people on knees. One trying to block the noise.

Memorialize, remember
under arch of Titus, blink,
crush Jews of Palestine, cart
their treasure

Thrown from god
to scientific study
to dissection
of our bodies
this is how it works

The knife in the
right place

At work speak
accordingly

The books, the records, the will, the words

Cain, Abel   Romulus, Remus

Commissioned
to create
gold doors

28 scenes
in quatrefoils

Ruler of Judea, Herod Antipas
encouraged by his wife
arrests St. John

Later
Salome
Herod's stepdaughter
serpentines dance floor
Herod entranced
offers
any
request

Salome persuaded
by her mother
asks for St. John's
head
on a platter

The poles hold art
the square floors
contain bodies
where I go walking

At top of the city
triangle of life
below
shops are tiny
store windows'
hand-colored soaps
cupcakes
real world items
money in your pocket
hanger   hanger

Nothing terrifying disturbs the maze

Enter

Space
surrounds

Velvet chair
transparent gowns
halos
paint shimmers canvas
cloths embrace waists
immaculate sheets
the trees exhumed
light and wind left no mark

They were called up
the dirty lot
blamed
much like Africans
who are said
to create
their graves
and die and die
whose hollow
faces are
shamed
to campaign
it was in those years
it spread
killing half of Florence
Siena   think of all
the temples
canvases
vacant
the smell
it could only
be from
the greatest
evil
the blood
drinkers
the money
users
the rats
the fleas
them

Boys threw rocks
marched military steps
sang praise collected
donations

Michelangelo's brother burned paintings
Botticelli threw his
away

Savonarola
tortured
burned

The fire sixty feet high
people's faces flushed

The crowd demanded a miracle
from the fire
two fingers curled

The crowd ran
horrified
glorified
crushing each other
to death

Brown plains
below the precipice
cracks and falls reminiscent of convulsions
to be looked at with desperation
words placed to the movement
security unclips, clatters

Immersed in sunlight
wear white clothes
old pine trees
scroll across
buildings

Dante
the great hook

Depletion=Art
=

Vow to be perfect
rescind my flaws
burn in the forest
eaten by birds

FOUR

Foot's bone pushing through
walking beside older self, resigned to immediate pulses
compliant
anaerobic speck in a jar
a tiny hole with water

Hands held toward sky
who's to help paper cut figures
a line of them trails off
each with a worse condition than the last
red lit spots suggest sores on the body
become illuminated by these zones

I should go to an ocean
hunt for water so I can sleep
everything sheer
I have an image of ocean
in me
poke the stick
dig
the salt
kelp blue
barnacle

Should images be retouched
the pink glow
compound properties
are inconspicuous

Go back where body went
concave in the sand
eyes draw in color

Standing at a table, pinky extended
downed a cappuccino, bit from a
croissant and then
a terrible day
the tape in me ripped
curled brown
hung from my chest

The smoke and smell are killing
standing too close to tables
collapsing

Can't hear clipped woman in geometric hair
blonde shaggy
ice blue eyes, innocuous
"We're in World War Three it's happening"
jeans shifted up by belt loops
"and he is doing a fine job leading"

A woman asks about animals
stacked carcasses, fur rigid with blood
she left her daughter
unafraid to fly
the guide is flippant
this edifice is profound with the right
perception do you know what was
negotiated in the Pantheon significant work
on the ceiling
stare at it until your eyes water
'til it pillows to your sight
to be this sick is inconvenient
a weary traveler is taboo
rooms stapled down barely there
this room is all bed
heat turned to the wind
together they push you
I will be careful not to soil the lens
if you write in this journal
the water fountain isn't lovely
I suppose a picture of the lion would be just
the bread is wet
corridors effuse the feeling of night

              old ways
              in effect

killings old style

                repeat ourselves

habit creatures

                were they gone from work

papers said
everyone suspect

                one leader evil
                the other a hawk

appraisals depend on group
you join

                detectives cloud screen
                blood leaks
                there's work to be done

you think I could
dissociate
or is that also
a move-
ment

last language
retold
from
other
mouth

monuments
memorials
pantheons
coliseums

bodies, torpedoes
clothes flip
voluntarily

Hide
under its bridge
run for the capital R
swim in its belly
it stands tall
beckons
so do
gold walls
marble finger
airplane
solace is where
I'm asking the
question
row in Romance
crack open
let red shell
dry

The cloud's outline
defines itself

A kiss is a ghost
is a branch
is raking

Eyes closed
out come more stories

The idea is to love wholly
a punctured tube bleeds
red, yellow, green
[smear]

Ancient intellectualizing

Abstracts
depend on my life

Ink scrawls a message
let love be animals, weeds

FIVE

Away it is creeping to find out what to do
It tunnels to a home that burns at the tip
Art barely gave
Sand was vast

All vacations fused

Red flags disappeared
There was wheat and fog

Those with me
illuminated separately
they want to appreciate
what is to be observed

Bushes
carry wetness

Shiny cars on gravel

Fingers tight at stem of glass
red legs   crawl

Chocolate earth bouquet

A collie bites

Bottles boxed and tucked

Envisioned by artists

A city

Space
where
sunkeness
takes
room
birds
shooting
through
the
fence's
hole
impeccable

pulled
from
itineraries
television
in
another
language
images
weren't
translatable

mopeds
continued
cheese
was
sold
began
to
think
of
breakfast

we
were
trying
not
to
read
where
to
eat
at
least
in
mornings
where
we'd
form
a
cue
with
others
eat
off
small
plates

now
sister
and
brother
must
be
found
ring

the
bell
blow
my
horn
the
dress
I
wear
red
flounders
in
the
wind

roll
over
map
the
line

it
is
lucky
I
saved
crackers
in
my
purse

over
dinner
Canadians
show
us
which
pastas
to
eat

wine
starch

there
is
no
way
to
talk
about
trauma
inferences
circumvent
the
general
talk

Back in the hills   earth tone   a bell tower
crags

Ponte Vecchio   loops over water   streets merge
at each end

Dante
thorny crown
vulture in shadow

Michelangelo's sarcophagus   slabs of white marble
three angels
one doesn't hold back
arches over   silk falls

Stone gets me
more than painting
faces serene   blank   horrified

Other images
felt visited
always something letting you down:
at the artifact breath held
you whistled it out
assuming there was more
you were missing
when you rode up on the boat to the lady in green
holding the torch
that—

Where were abstract painters at the time of decadence
where could one go with differences
lack of funds
and not being a crowd pleaser

Mary in every face angle
the baby clutched emphatically

The white world and the very black
the blondes and the blues

Panorama of Gucci, Prada, legs, waist
smoke and butter funneled to a rich scene

Are you looking in—
washing glass that's dirty

In our modern ways we redefine
present, project
re-exhibit
and with showings upcoming
being seasoned appropriately
redefinition is only definition
another set course to follow
and eat as the flock gets ready for take off
the glass kindly washed again

Back again to you and I
as if we jumped from the pages
as if we were
page numbers
disoriented, displaced
looking for the single file line

We are hated tremendously
so we hide in each other
a move to the left
contains knee and foot pains,
to the right
all others suffer

We unravel
in another city
in the cold cold woods

Space to move
where production
slows down

I can't lose my body. I'm membered by its attachments.
I will receive more blankets from her if I can find the house.
There is no phone. Her husband smiled and she had red hair
and that was that story. I am working on getting loose.
The cats in every direction appear aimless. The people
knocking at the door. No not available just yet but almost.
Perhaps it is the smell of water that is doing this. Perhaps with
culture everything can heal. The hole will shrink.

SIX

You were first up the bell tower's 400 stairs
it was starred in the book
we are diligent about stars

The top broke to an expanse
that couldn't be interpreted
so it remained there
and I here

Marble ices floors and sculptures
there is a spin   take it in

Stairs down to back rooms   candle lit
Jesus grabbing Mary's breast
propels it towards onlookers   the woman calls: "Is it worth
going down these steps
are the bottom rooms worth it?"

We motioned forward
paused at the bronze she-wolf
stunned by infinite mosaic floors
a skull in a lit box

With rules comes disjointedness   what have we replaced
with physical rebuking

Francis with a collection of birds
Francis

These birds are ravishing my feet
ravishing

fill carafe to mouth
red ring on tablecloth

                            everything brown
                            walking edges
                            broken glass pane
                            black cat revealed

              wet stone
              barred windows
              arched wall
              buildings flat

all houses brown
look down
no depth to roofs
overlapping cards
like a movie where
everything flits
where wings jostle
pass a roll

spread butter
devour
everyone hides smiles
wears outfits
knows we are strangers

Found on a page written by you
the feeling was to pass it quickly
but that is what most would do
why out of a book of words
would you encroach what I was
thinking
little black bones stare out on
the page
taking home briefly
the weather is suitable
I only bought
a scarf for my neck
I've yet to see the water

Lights darken
tingle to themselves
small insects
invisible

Today:
blank:
American guide says
courtesan
we stare at Botticellis
gold bracelets stack
against wrist

On tour
five balls
and top window
myth of princess who never really died
black bird on Sabine
writing down
where to get good
bracelets

Top of city
on a bus
with no ticket
buried in the back

One tells us her business
they all want to:
another small town
hill town   small town
little gem
maybe one we didn't know

Must stay in monastery
lights out at ten

City lights bobbing
beneath
the setting wails
the perfect night

become sound
undoubtedly collecting
crooked identity
a building
a street
walking below
overlapping color
no skin tones
features
XXX
paste squares

this is where I stop

Loose dirt between gardened areas

The yellow fish slipped through her fingers
but the feel of water was on her skin

Everything shaken
perfect mobiles

Activity's a time-running antidote

Printed in the United States
136452LV00002BA/3/P